THE CRONE'S FLAME:
Radiance Made Flesh

THE CRONE'S FLAME:
Radiance Made Flesh

Copyright ©2025 by Betsey Grobecker
betgrobecker@gmail.com

Cover photograph by Melissa Fanton
Cover design by Debbi Wraga

All rights reserved

ISBN Number: 978-1-60571-693-0

Printed in the United States of America

THE CRONE'S FLAME:
Radiance Made Flesh

Betsey Grobecker

The Crone's Flame of Destruction:
Burning the Knotted Veil of Separation

I Am You, as You,
but you insist you are your earthly identity.

I Am You, as You,
but you will not feel the tone of Radiance's Beauty
singing within and about you.

I Am You, as You,
but you do not breathe the free-flowing breath of Grace
dancing through the hollow bones of your frame.

I Am a witness to your suffering,
as you remain caged by rules
sourced from outside of you.

I Am a witness to your pain,
as you defend the beliefs of your identity,
ceaselessly searching for meaning and fulfillment.

The Crone's Flame: Radiance Made Flesh

I Am a witness to your breakdown,
as all you held sacred shatters to the ground,
and the old structures can no longer hold your bones in place.

I Am the groundless ground,
honoring the surrendered offerings of your ancestry,
while opening My womb to cradle and receive you.

I Am the burn of My compassionate Flame,
transmuting your suffering into Love
within the alchemical blood of My womb.

I Am the You.
You are becoming.

One

I was sitting on my deck overlooking Lake Erie, even though the night was hot and the air heavy with smoke. The fires and scorching heat had kept most people inside for weeks, but I could no longer find space to breathe within enclosed walls. Tonight, I disregarded the weather alerts.

The reddish-orange sun sank into the horizon, its Flame descending on a parched Earth that had not felt a drop of rain in almost two months. Water restrictions, imposed weeks earlier, had split the soil into deepening crevices—its once lush green carpet now brittle straw that pierced the soles of my feet. The scent of burnt, listless life scratched my throat. No matter how much I drank, I could not quench my thirst. Even my skin cried out for moisture, unmoved by cold showers or lotions. My eyes burned with the same flame that scorched the Earth.

I raised my gaze to the sun, daring it to soften. It only mocked me, searing my eyes with its red-hot reflection. "Do you even give a damn?!" I screamed.

Irritability burned away my easy-going nature. Tempers flared everywhere. The old courtesies—once masking shame behind polite masks—were dissolving in the heat. No one had the patience for niceties anymore. Guilt gave way to raw nerves and the primal urge to survive each day.

When the burning sun finally yielded to darkness, the air remained heavy and hot. The haze blurred the moon's reflection on the water, and I sobbed for the loss of the beauty that once offered peace. As nature died around me, so too did the part of me that knew how to meet it with reverence. I retreated indoors, grateful at least for the dream world and the cool refuge of home.

I awoke choking, my breath clawing for oxygen through the thick, fetid air. The smoke alarm shrieked. In the blackness, I stumbled over furniture, searching for the door. Outside, neighbors ran in panic. The night screamed with gasping breaths, choking coughs, and piercing cries—grief spilling in every direction. My own voice joined the chaos, howling with pain and terror.

The fire roared its triumph, its ferocity stirring the still air into a wild tornado that tore the scaffolding of our homes to pieces. The fire hoses were no match; water turned to steam before it could soothe the blaze.

Then someone screamed, "Lucinda!" and her black eyes, full of immense compassion, flashed in my memory. My panic surged beyond the space my body could hold. My dearest friend. My mentor. Lucinda—where was she? Her name joined my howls as I ran toward the flame. Only when my daughter grabbed my arm did I realize she was beside me. She clung to my smoke-drenched body, but nothing could quell the rage that tore through me.

My screams ripped open—raw and bleeding. Through smoke-ravaged eyes I searched the fire, and a dragon rose from within it. Its hissing breath gave no chance—nothing could escape death. The blood thickened in my throat, and I roared it toward the beast.

My breath merged with the dragon's—we roared fire into a space unbound by direction. My breath was the dragon's breath. My gaze, the dragon's gaze. I dared the sun to mock me now.

Then—the water in the fire hoses turned to blood. A dark red liquid covered our fiery breath with its thickness. Our breath yielded to this liquid, allowing its eerie calm to absorb its fury. Its soothing warmth flowed beneath my bare feet, and Earth's deep cracks drank the blood with reverent thirst.

I closed my burning eyes—too dry for tears—and breathed as deeply as my scorched lungs allowed. Every pore of my skin expanded to drink this soothing liquid. The strength in my legs gave way, and I surrendered my body to Earth's body. Its blood-filled crevices opened to cradle me, and I descended into Her womb.

A darkness of luminous light lit the space of my existence. Yet no sun and no lamps illuminated it. The light seemed to emanate from space itself, needing nothing beyond itself to shine.

I lay upon a lush green carpet of ground, a vast stillness filling me. I had no idea where my body rested, but I was empty of fear. The "where" of this place held no importance.

The fragrance of greenery—of nature's deep, unspeakable beauty—swirled about me in the breeze. I closed my eyes and breathed it in, drawing it deep into the crevices of a mind and body that had felt lifeless. Swirls of dancing light, radiant with joy, moved through me. I giggled with blissful acknowledgement, then breathed deeply to welcome it.

Pain groaned from within the marrow of my bones, and tears of blood spilled from my eyes. I let them flow, unafraid. They were tears of release—of what I did not know, nor did I need to. Nothing mattered but this clean, joyful play of light breathing into every hidden space of my being.

The groans continued. I joined them as we groaned with the pain of release. A cracking sound rang out, and for a flash, I saw space within my bones open as debris dislodged. Compassion—so deep it felt ancient—saturated the blood flowing from my eyes, loosening the knots of my memory even further. I knew only the pulse of this profound Love, a Love that accepted all that had been, exactly as it was.

I surrendered all of me to this Love, offering it the breath of my life. And as It loved me through my surrendered breath, our shared breath was making Love to everything I had battled—everything I could not accept about myself.

Oh, how I breathed this exquisite breath of Love. I drank it into every cell, and into the space beyond the cells, until even the marrow of my bones moaned with pleasure. The twisted knots of ancestral pain—and my own pain born through them—began to dissolve. Everything melted into a breath of pure light, hollowing out the hardened roots of memory within the skeleton of my being.

When the exhaustion of release reached its peak, I rested. I rested in a space of peace I had never known.

A gentle lapping of water reached my ears. I turned my head toward the sound and saw a lake shimmering with luminous, pulsing light. It beckoned me to come play. I didn't want to move from my place of absolute rest—but how could I not respond to such beauty?

The Crone's Flame: Radiance Made Flesh

I laughed as I sat up, surprised at the lack of gravity in the movement. "My bones must appreciate the relief," I thought. My joints, usually stiff, now moved freely. I had been in this body for sixty-one years, and it no longer had the flexibility it once had. I supposed my bones had absorbed their share of "gunk" over the years, clogging their ease.

I bent over to peer at the lake's surface. Its playful light dancing on the crystal-clear water enchanted me. My reflection wore a veil of smoke, and my throat held a rawness. Fire flashed across my memory, but my breath carried no grief, no tension of tragedy. Instead, it pulsed with a knowing—beyond reason, beyond form—saturated in a divine fragrance.

And in that pulse, I laughed softly, whispering:

I Am, and that is divine comedy enough.

Do not linger in the mind's unraveling of these words, for the laughter is not of reason but of Radiance remembering Itself.

Still smiling, I removed the clothing that still carried the smell of death and stepped into the water. My dry skin absorbed this crystalline water into the very fabric of its cells—and deeper still, into a space newly opened for Love to breathe. The cells of my skin celebrated their new freedom as this magical water pulsed through them.

I giggled, then offered the water to my throat. The dried blood of my past howls flowed through their newly found moisture—releasing a vibration, a voice, that had forgotten how to sing the love it now remembered.

As I sipped the lake's mysterious water, it became the blood of my bones' sobbing wounds. Its resonance sang a hauntingly beautiful song of love that etched itself deeper and deeper into the cellular memory of my being, lifting more debris from its hiding places. My yearning deepened. I wanted to know the full depth of this mysterious beauty.

Within the blood of my bones, I made a vow: I would give anything—everything—to unveil the essence of my Being.

Shimmers of light descended upon the lake's surface as I made my vow. In an instant, the lake became a whirlpool that absorbed the light into its depths. The swirling motion rippled through my bones, as if the lake was drawing the marrow of my wounds into the womb of its body. When the motion stilled, the crystalline waters once again radiated their quiet, pulsing Presence.

A ripple of transparent light spread across the lake, flowering into a spiral unlike anything I had ever known. It opened above the shore. From within the brilliance, the body of a woman appeared.

Her skin radiated such ecstasy that I could barely make out her form. Her being pulsed with exquisite Love and wisdom, moving through her body in a dance of pure joy. Her form and her body were nearly indistinguishable. She was radiant Love, making Love to itself through movement that defied all known laws of motion. Even her form defied form—she was a melding of all genders, all ages. The totality of life moved through her, even the wildness of nature.

Her flowing movement became a gaze—saturated with loving wisdom—her whole Presence a pulse of light flowing through and around her. Her gaze was a hollow cave of light, holding sun and moon within it—and something, or perhaps nothing, more sacred than either. The light in her eyes pulsed as a crystalline Presence. No color I knew could describe it.

"Welcome," is what I sensed her saying. I couldn't tell if her mouth moved. The word arrived as a resonance—a vibration heard beyond hearing. It was the tone of her welcome, more than any word.

"Hello. I hope I didn't disturb your dance of grace. Such profound beauty for me to witness."

A slight bow of light emanated from her pulsing form. "You are not the witness to my Beauty. You are this Beauty, Aware of Itself as Beauty."

Her words unsettled me. I could not dance with such indescribable grace—though now I yearned to. The Beauty she spoke of was unlike anything I knew. How could I be this Presence of such impossible Radiance?

"Oh no, you're quite mistaken. Unlike you, I have a body—solid, aching with the weight of age. I've never felt the Beauty you embody, let alone been it."

"Your bones are beginning to remember your Truth as you breathe Its loving wisdom into your mind and body. I see a small stream of light flowing through the blood in your bones. This light is already transmuting all that veils the grandeur of who You Are. Breathe deeply—feel my Beauty as your own."

Though I doubted her, I yearned to feel the majesty of the Presence before me. So I closed my eyes and breathed—deeper, deeper—until her Presence merged with my breath. My whole being opened, her unspeakable majesty pulsing through me. In one breath, resistance fell away, releasing into the depths of all I had forgotten.

Every cell in my body bellowed in bliss, and my body moved in joy. I danced—without pain—until I collapsed onto Earth. Maybe, just maybe, her Beauty could be mine, I mused, lying in joy. Yet she saw only a small stream of light in me—and my cells ached to embody the full depths of that Radiance.

I rose, reverent. "How can I turn this stream of light into a river?"

"By remembering the Radiance you sense is You. Eternal. Present everywhere. A blanket of radiating Love and wisdom. Breathe It through you—every moment you remember to. It will begin to dissolve the debris hidden deep in your wounded blood, no longer needed to support you.

"The energy of your mind will resist the Presence of Radiance—it fears for its survival. Don't fight your thoughts or let them rule you. Acknowledge them. Then remember You are Beauty. Breathe this Love into every speck of your mind and body. In time, your mind will surrender and learn to serve this Radiance."

As she spoke of my mind, confusion pierced the bliss, dimming the joy I'd felt. I reached for something solid—something that could anchor me.

"My name is Julia."

The moment I said it, memories surfaced—flavored with sweetness and ache. My life. My responsibilities. Julia. The fire returned, but this time, it brought the fear I had known, panic rising with each memory. Was this all a dream to escape my pain? No, I must wake. Face my life. I could not escape what waited for me.

"I need to go now," I said to a dimming light. "But I'd like to return when I can. I don't know how to find my way home—or how to return here. Can you help me?"

Her light dimmed further, and her voice dissolved into the fading resonance, barely comprehensible.

"The memories you choose will guide you. Will you cling to pain and fear born of the world? Or will you choose the loving wisdom that arises from your hollowing bones? You are not the charged, earthly identity of 'Julia.'

"You dream yourself awake, again and again—just as you're doing now. When will you dissolve into One who never sleeps?"

Evey crevice, every drop of blood within my bones shuddered, reminding me of my vow to always choose Love. But in my confusion, I could not yet remember what my bones already knew.

Right now, as I slipped back into time and space—I needed to be Julia.

"I am ... I am Julia. I have a daughter. I have a life I must return to." I kept repeating, anchoring myself in the name.

"Yes ... yes you are Julia," a voice echoed softly. "Julia—can you open your eyes and speak to me?"

Two

It began with a sound I could not name—low and resonant, as if my bones themselves were humming. At first, I thought it was the wind lacing through the branches outside, but no ... it was deeper than that. Older. It came from within, as though the marrow carried memory and had grown restless in the quiet.

Only my breath moved—slow, unforced. I let it settle into a space of ease. The quieter my breath became, the more still my thoughts grew, until there was only listening.

Somewhere in that silence, a weight I had carried without knowing began to loosen—just enough for me to feel its shape. It was not grief. Not exactly. It felt older than grief, older even than me. A pulse belonging to those who had come before, and to those who would follow after.

And then—I felt her. Not fully, only a flicker through the silence, as if Lucinda had passed through the room without stirring the air. No words. Only the faintest shift, like the pull of an unseen tide pulling me inward.

The hum deepened. I closed my eyes. Something in me was listening that did not need ears. My breath began to move like the waning tide that gathers the storm's debris and carries it into the ocean's belly for renewal. Threads of the moon's soft golden light wove into small streams flowing through my bones. They hummed lullabies that invited me to hear the mysteries my ancient bones had sung for eternity.

"Beneath the layering of your pain, the pulse of Beauty, as You, sings. Breathe with the tides within you. Relax your mind and breathe the golden waters as they move through you. These waters know your bones; they cleanse what history could not."

I felt the Truth in their voice. I smelled the sweet fragrance of an ancient memory—free of ceaseless noise, of judgment, of shame. And I dimly recalled a vow I had once taken: to breathe the breath of this memory through every fiber of my being, always. I sobbed, knowing I had lost something of great Beauty that I yearned to become. And yet, I did not know the substance of this memory. I knew only the substance of my Earth life as Julia.

Flashes of memory—joyful, painful, and all shades in between—rose before me as the golden waters bathed them in Love. The powers that clung to me, choking my breath, loosened but did not fully yield. A fear pressed against my chest like a wall—the kind that clenches the breath and makes the bones ache for what is familiar, even when the familiar is heavy.

"Really?" I whispered into the silence, amused by the mind's smallness. The wall quivered, and I felt the marrow laugh gently:

The Crone's Flame: Radiance Made Flesh

I Am, and that is divine comedy enough.

"Mom, are you OK? Why are you crying?"

My daughter's voice startled me. She had returned from work. I have been at her home for a couple of weeks now. Next week, I plan to begin looking for a place of my own.

I peered into the worry of her hazel eyes. Only then did I notice how the brightness of her childhood gaze had dimmed. I wondered if my eyes, too, were dim—or did they hold light? Had I only dreamed they were made of light?

My tears had soaked into my skin. I brushed away the remnants; they felt oddly sacred, like the salty blood of the ocean's belly tenderly washing my wounds.

"Yes, yes, I'm fine," I told her softly. "Just releasing some old sorrow. No worries."

Linda's eyes filled with more concern. My words no longer left me as quickly as they once had. Each seemed to pause, weighing itself in silence before crossing my lips. I had touched something of great Beauty during the fire—something elusive.

She was about to speak, but I gave her a look, and she bit her tongue. She believed I was unwell and should stay longer. But I knew the Truth; while I was weepy and disoriented, I was well.

My own space would reveal itself soon—a space nearer the quiet hum of trees and open sky. The world I once chased—its demands, its noise, its luxuries—no longer called to me. What I longed for now had no name, yet I could feel it, the way I felt the tide breathing within me. And even as I let go of my teaching career, life was already drawing me toward something new.

Two weeks had passed since Lucinda's death, and the invitation to celebrate her life rested on the kitchen counter. I did not know what I would feel there—only that I had to go.

The tide within me had quieted to a steady hum by morning—a soft drum sounding beneath the ribs. I sat for a long time, hands wrapped around a cup of tea, watching the thin veil of steam rising into the air as if it carried whispers I was not yet ready to hear.

Linda's voice, warm but cautious, drew me back.

"Mom? Don't forget about today."

Today. The word landed with a weight that was not heavy, but undeniable. Lucinda's gathering. Two weeks since her passing, and yet her Presence felt nearer than ever. It wasn't a funeral, Linda had reminded me more than once. It was a celebration—a circle of those who loved her, sharing stories, laughter, and the strange ache that comes when beauty and loss meet in the same breath.

Beauty—that was her very essence. Being with her was like sitting in sunlight without ever feeling scorched. And yet, only now did I truly *feel* the Radiance that had always gleamed from her black, peaceful eyes. How had I missed something so pure?

I heard Linda's sigh when I didn't answer and simply nodded, my voice remaining silent. It preferred silence now. In silence, I could feel the golden waters moving through my bones. Yet another part of me—older, bone-deep—knew I had to step into the world again. Not as I had been; that old persona was faltering. But as someone I was only beginning to become.

The Crone's Flame: Radiance Made Flesh

I dressed slowly, as if each button and fold of fabric were roots grounding me back into the life that once wore these clothes. Even so, I felt the shimmer—faint, persistent—like moonlight keeping the tides aglow. I did not want to lose it.

Before leaving, I pressed my palm against the doorframe and closed my eyes. "I will carry you," I whispered—not to Lucinda, but to the vow, the waters, the unseen tides singing their ancient tones within me. Then I opened the door, knowing I was crossing more than one threshold.

The late-morning light, warm without intensity, softened my edges of anticipation. Linda touched my shoulder, a quiet reassurance, as we walked to the car. I wondered if she could feel it too—the hum that had never left me, the sense that this gathering was not about Lucinda's past, but about something quietly awakening within me.

We drove in a silence that allowed its secrets to be heard. I listened.

The house where Lucinda had lived most of her life stood at the edge of town, tucked against a grove of old oaks whose branches arched like guardians. By the time we arrived, the driveway was already lined with cars, their windows flashing the sun's muted shimmer.

At the door, I hesitated, my hand resting on the weathered wood. Laughter—woven with tones of grief that tried to smile—drifted from inside.

Within, lamplight glowed against the scent of cedar. Friends and family moved in gentle currents, embracing, murmuring, sharing memories that rose and fell like tides. On the mantel, Lucinda's photograph rested between two white candles. Her eyes, caught in the frozen frame, still held that same quiet mischief, as though she knew something the rest of us had yet to discover.

I gazed deeply into her eyes—perhaps for the first time—and felt a glimmer of her mischief. It teased me, drawing me into the depths of her hidden eyes and, for an instant, into the depths of my own. I turned away, not from fear, but from the ache of recognition. How could a photograph feel so alive?

Linda squeezed my hand before joining a cluster of relatives. I lingered at the edge, not ready to step fully in. My breath came shallow at first—but then I felt it: the shimmer, faint but certain, moonlight spilling through my bones.

I moved slowly among the voices and embraces. Then, without fanfare, I felt her. Not in sight, not in sound, but in a way marrow knows the tide. Lucinda. A warm fragrance of Presence, light as breath. The shimmer deepened, humming through my bones as I gazed into her photograph.

One of her friends began to speak. "Lucinda used to say," the woman laughed softly, wiping tears from her cheeks, "When life cracks you open, don't patch it up too fast. Let the light pierce you first."

The room stilled, as if those words had landed on every heart at once. The shimmer in me swelled. It was not memory. It was *her*.

I closed my eyes briefly, and there she was—not in form, but as vastness. She was the tide, the Radiance, the breath without edges.

I exhaled, long and slow. I was not here only to honor her. I was here because something in me had begun to breathe—the same luminous tide she had carried, now stirring awake in my own bones.

As the gathering thinned, I lingered near the photograph. Lucinda's eyes—dark, unhurried, shimmering with mischief—gestured for me to play along. My heart smiled, and the shimmer in her eyes seemed to brighten. I felt them say, "Finally, your heart is beginning to flower into the light of your Truth."

I Am, and that is divine comedy enough.

I touched the frame—not to claim her, but to let the tide within me flow to greet her Presence. "Thank you," I whispered, though my voice barely sounded.

Stepping outside, the air felt different. The sun was descending, a breeze moving through leaves as if to exhale with me. Linda's hand rested gently on my arm, grounding me. Beneath her touch, another current stirred—one with roots deep into the womb of Earth, as steadfast as the trees anchored in Her pulsing belly.

On the drive home, I leaned into the quiet between us, Lucinda's friend's words still echoing: *When life cracks you open, don't patch it up too fast. Let the light pierce you first.*

I did not know yet what this light was. But I could feel it—faint, steady, like a tide brushing a hidden shore. And somewhere deep in that tide, beyond name, beyond memory, an essence was awakening.

This time, I did not turn away.

That night, I dreamed of water moving through bone. No sound, no shape—only the pulse of something ancient, steady, and unafraid. When I woke, I could not name it, but I knew this: I was no longer standing at the edge of what was ending. I had stepped—unseen, unmeasured—into the beginning of what was remembering Me.

The Crone's Flame of Remembrance: The Tide Beneath All Things

Not a fire that burns to ash,
but one that reveals the bones
beneath the splintering masks.

She does not shout.
She hums.

And in her hum,
the marrow remembers its song.

The Crone's Flame: Radiance Made Flesh

This is not madness,
though the mind will call it so.

It is the undoing of forgetting—
a slow, inexorable light
licking through the hollows
where you thought you had lost yourself.

And in that song,
nothing is lost—only remembered.

Three

The morning after Lucinda's gathering, the hum within me had not quieted. If anything, it had deepened—less like a sound now and more like a Presence. An echo of something that had been waiting all my life.

I sat at the kitchen table with my hands wrapped around a cup of tea gone lukewarm. Outside, the world looked unchanged—bare trees, gray sky, a few stray leaves skipping across the lawn. Yet none of it felt ordinary anymore. Something unseen breathed beneath the surface of everything, as if life itself was revealing its majestic Presence and inviting me to notice.

A giggle almost rose from my throat, but it caught there. The part of me that had once clung to calendars, work schedules, and polite predictability had begun to crack. What seeped through the fractures was both terrifying and beautiful.

I didn't tell Linda. She was already watching me with quiet worry. I could feel her unasked questions in every glance, and I couldn't answer them even if I tried to. How could I explain that the ordinary world was thinning, that the edge between seen and unseen was dissolving? That the unseen was a mysterious, deep beauty calling me to awaken? That everything I once found alluring now felt pale?

I rose and walked to the window. The sky was a washed-out blue, like the dreams I'd held before the fire. Searching its muted hues for light, I caught a shimmer—faint, like moonlight lingering in daylight. The wind caught the leaves—and my breath—loosening, deepening, lifting it into their graceful currents.

Then it came. Not a vision. Not a voice. A memory.

A memory not mine alone. Beyond the memories I had cherished.

Fire—not the fire that took my home, but another fire—older and vaster. The kind that strips bare without destroying. A fire that knows bones.

Its sensation rippled across me like wind on still water. I gripped the windowsill, trembling—not from fear, but from recognition. I knew this fire. I let the world blur.

And then, as if whispered through the marrow itself:

You are not losing yourself. You are remembering.

I Am, and that is divine comedy enough.

I closed my eyes, breathing into the tone those words carried, rooting their song into Earth's belly … or was it my own?

Behind me, Linda's footsteps crossed the kitchen. "Mom," she said softly. "I made breakfast. You should eat something."

I turned and gave her a quiet smile—the kind that carried both worlds in it.

"I will."

The tide of remembrance was still moving within me. I knew I would follow it, wherever it led.

The hum no longer felt foreign. It was becoming familiar—a pulse of profound silence, revealed only when I was no longer breathing the shallow breath of worldly chatter. Soft, elongated breaths of Love moved me into the stillness where the pulse sang.

That afternoon, I walked in a nearby park. Bare branches stretched toward the sky as if to drink in every available ray of light. The air was crisp with winter's quiet—but it was a quiet full of Presence, as though Earth Herself was breathing beneath my feet.

I paused by an old oak whose trunk bore the scars of centuries. Placing my palm against the bark, I closed my eyes. There it was again: the low, steady hum—not from the tree, not from me, but from the place we shared.

And then I heard it—faint, like the first note of a song carried from far away:

The marrow remembers. The roots remember. The breath remembers.

I Am, and that is divine comedy enough.

I opened my eyes, the world shimmered—not with light, but with Presence.

Lucinda's fragrance touched me. Her laughter—light, fearless. Her eyes, compassionate yet glimmering with mischief, unsettled and comforted me at once. And I knew: my grief was not clinging to what I had lost. It was a graceful surrender, honoring the past so I could step into ancient memory that had always been waiting.

When I returned home, Linda was reading on the couch. She looked up with a question in her eyes but didn't ask it. Maybe she could feel it too—that something in me was shifting, like the slow turning of a tide.

I sat beside her in silence, letting the hum move through me like a hidden current. For the first time in years, I felt no need to explain myself. I only needed to listen.

Beneath that listening, I sensed it—a quiet pull. A whisper of life humming in dense woods, in crystalline waters untouched by time, of wild spaces unknown to walls and clocks. And the pulse of that life called to me.

That night, as sleep began to blur the edges of thought, I saw it—just for a moment: a cabin cradled by trees, its windows spilling light in silent welcome. I didn't reach for it. I simply breathed and let it be.

And in that letting be, the hum deepened, as if it had been waiting for this quiet all along.

The hum lingered, steady as breath.

In the days that followed, I began noticing spaces I'd never known existed—the pause between a bird's call and its echo, the hollow hush of snow-laden air, the stillness of my own heartbeat at night. Even the darkness of night teased me with faint shimmers of light pulsing from within it.

It was no longer enough to walk the neighborhood paths. The pull toward something wilder, quieter, grew stronger.

One morning, as Linda sipped her coffee and scrolled her phone, I heard myself say, "I think I'm ready to find a place of my own. Somewhere … quieter."

She looked up, startled but not surprised. "Out of town?"

The Crone's Flame: Radiance Made Flesh

"Further," I said, my hand settling over my chest where the hum now lived. "Closer to the woods. Maybe by water."

Linda's brow furrowed with worry, but she offered no protest. "If that's what you need. ..."

That night, I dreamed of the cabin again—same one cradled by trees, light spilling from its windows in a warm, wordless welcome. This time, I did not hold back. I let my heart receive the light.

I stepped closer, though my feet did not move. The hum carried me, as if something ancient coiled deep in my marrow had unfurled its wings to guide me forward. I felt its slow, sinuous Presence—like a dragon asleep for centuries, now awakening—not to frighten, but to carry me across a threshold. Its breath was the same hum that had been with me all along, only now I knew its source.

I vaguely remembered moving like this before—dancing through a lightness as an unknown essence flowed through me.

When I woke, I lay still, my breath long and slow. The image of the cabin didn't fade.

It was not just a dream.

It was a remembering.

And somewhere deep inside, I knew:

It was almost time to go.

Four

On the morning of a life turning toward the unknown, even the sky seemed to mirror the change—soft gray, still as a held breath. I stood in Linda's driveway, hands wrapped around a thermos of tea, watching my breath curl into the chill. The winter wind felt oddly still for winter, as if it, too, was holding its breath. I glanced at Linda who was uncharacteristically still, as though she, too, were waiting.

Linda was loading the last of my belongings into the car. I felt our bond shift—still strong, but looser now. I hadn't realized how much I'd leaned on her love until I sensed that grip beginning to release.

"Are you sure you'll be okay out there?" she asked. Her voice carried a worry, but in her eyes was something quieter—resignation, and perhaps a faint glimmer of understanding she could not yet name.

"Yes," I said. My voice was soft, yet steady. We were both changing. The dependence that had once woven itself between us was yielding to something that could make us stronger—each in our own way.

The drive was long. Silence suited it. The noise of towns and traffic fell away, replaced by winding roads edged with frozen fields and stands of skeletal trees. Beneath that quiet, I could hear the hum of the land singing through my chest, tuning me to its hidden rhythm.

The cabin caught my breath when it came into view. It was exactly as I'd seen it in my dreams—tucked among the trees, wrapped in stillness that felt almost alive, as if it had been waiting for me all along. Snow blanketed the roof and clung to the windowpanes. A thin curl of smoke drifted from the chimney, carrying the faint, resin-sweet scent of cedar into the crisp air.

I stepped out of the car. The hush of the woods was not empty—it was fullness. Even the crunch of my boots on the snow seemed loud in its vastness.

Placing my hand on the cabin door, I felt it: the hum. No longer faint, but resonant, like a low, ancient drum sounding through my bones. Without hesitation, I turned the key and stepped inside.

The air smelled of cedar and something else I could not name, a fragrance that stirred the same warmth as the dream-light pouring from these windows. I set my bags down and stood in the center of the room.

And I heard it—not with my ears, but as though the walls themselves were speaking: The marrow remembers.

I Am, and that is divine comedy enough.

I closed my eyes, pressed my palm to my chest, and breathed. For the first time, I wasn't searching for home.

I was standing in it.

That night, I lay in the small bed at the far end of the cabin. I kept the lamp off, not out of thrift or habit, but because I welcomed the dark. The glow of cities and towns, once a comfort, had long since become a veil over the living silence I craved.

Through the window, the forest stood like a cathedral. Its branches etched black against the faint silver wash of moonlight. My gaze settled there, and my breath fell into the slow rhythm of its stillness. The hum began to weave itself through me again—steady, patient, unrelenting in its quiet Love.

The darkness here was not an absence, nor did it carry the loneliness I'd once felt in shadowed rooms. It was alive, pulsing with a Radiance too subtle for ordinary eyes. I could feel it in the floorboards, in the cedar-scented walls, in the steady song of my own bones. The whole cabin breathed with me, drawing me inward, until thought dissolved into a hum.

"I remember," I whispered into the quiet.

No reply came. Yet the hum deepened, and that deepening was enough. Night's warmth—vast, starless, infinite—wrapped around me. I curled beneath the quilt, not from weariness, but in a deep surrender so complete it erased the last boundaries between myself and the living dark.

Just before sleep took me, I saw it—not a dream, but a shimmer of light within the blackness, moving like water over stone, beckoning me into its tide. For the first time, I didn't resist.

I felt it carry me.

The Crone's Flame of Integration:
Returning the Forgotten Song of Wholeness

The dragon's fire no longer scorches
in your merging breath.
You have heard Love's pulsing tone
in the marrow of your bones,
and your hollowed bones
have opened to receive Its Beauty.

Your breath attunes itself to a finer rhythm—
singing the pure tones
of Radiant Wisdom and Love.
Male, female, trans, young, old, bound by creed or rank …
you know these veils of friction no longer serve you.

The Crone's Flame: Radiance Made Flesh

Walk the steps of graceful surrender
into your inner depths.
Allow birth, expansion and death
to dissolve into Beauty.
You are the elegant simplicity of Radiant Wholeness.
There is No-thing more, and yet, every-thing beyond.

Breathe My Flame of Integration.

Five

And so the marrow opens, and the song becomes flesh.

The morning air stirred gently through the trees—a stillness holding a pulse that listens from a depth beyond human frequencies. I stood barefoot on the porch, a mug of warm tea in hand, sensing the groan of the wood beneath my awakening. I hadn't yet lit a fire. The coolness held a softness, a gentle illumination, tingling my skin like a memory surfacing from long ago.

My sleep had been deep—not the sleep of exhaustion, but of arrival. My body knew it had found Home, a resonance with the Beauty I was remembering. The hum remained present, moving as a current woven into my breath. No longer calling from a distance, it now pulsed within me, as Me.

Inside the cabin, half-unpacked boxes waited. I felt no urgency. The chair by the window, the worn table, the old kettle—each greeted me like a long-lost friend. Every object resonated with a silence, a sacredness born not from use, but from Presence.

I touched the table's surface, releasing my fingers into the depths of the songs it wanted to hum into my skin.

The Crone's Flame of Integration

"I remember you," I whispered—though I didn't know what memory had surfaced. It wasn't of a lifetime, but of a state of Being I had once known, long before name or form.

The forest, the hum in the stillness, the cabin, the soil beneath it—none of it was new. They were the same Presence I had always carried, now made visible. The old habit of chasing visions and decoding dreams softened in the fragrance of the morning air. I had only to listen.

And so I did.

I sat on the step, closed my eyes, and let the Earth's breath rise through my spine. The soft pulse of roots and the quiet murmur of unseen waters far beneath the soil flowed with my effortless breath. In that stillness, a truth surfaced:

You were never separate from the Beauty you sought.

I Am, and that is divine comedy enough.

The world of measured time lost its grip. Shadows blended with the sunlight across the floor. The scent of the changing wind softened from winter's growl as it welcomed spring's arrival. Birdsong shifted from morning's brightness to dusk's calm, now speaking the voice of time. At moments, time vanished altogether in the silence between two breaths.

Deep shifts stirred in me—beyond analysis, beyond what the past could understand. The harmonies of nature were a constant Presence, their songs soothing the edge of discomfort. The unfinished boxes remained, but they no longer called to be emptied. I was unpacking something else—what no longer served the essence awakening within me.

Hurry had no meaning here. My former routines were dissolving. I was beginning to live by the quiet rhythm of Being. My movements arose from a loving breath untouched by the past.

One morning, a whisper within the breeze beckoned me to a clearing at the forest's edge. I didn't question it. I stilled my thoughts and felt its invitation. The ground softened beneath my feet, moss receiving the weight I released into it. The trees, tall and silent, bore witness without demand.

As I walked, the air thickened into a sacred hush. The forest shimmered as a Presence I had already felt—the hum. A hum so beautiful it surrounded all. The forest itself was remembering with me.

Light spilled through the canopy like liquid breath, rooting me in place. The scent of damp Earth, faint woodsmoke, and something wilder—unnamable—swirled around me.

A hollow-based tree caught my attention. I knelt before it, pressing my palm against its bark. And there it was:

I call back the song of my bone marrow.

The words rose from the hollow space within my bones, remembered through the soil. No incarnation. No striving. Just a transparent recognition. A return.

Tears did not flow this time. The grief had been carried away long ago. Only stillness remained ... the pulse of Radiance remembered in form. Yet beneath that stillness, I felt it: the slow coil of something ancient, resting deep within, as if a dragon had curled Itself inside my marrow to guard what was awakening.

Space opened all about me.

A space pulsing with such immense Love that my body could not move. I gave the totality of my weight to the Earth. Eyes closed, I breathed the fragrance of sacredness into my depths, feeling the voice of the vow that my blood had always carried. The hollow at the base of the tree mirrored the deepening hollow of my bones.

When I had enough presence in my body to move again, I sat at its base. Leaning into the tree's ancient curve, I felt the echo of memories woven into the bark's quiet hush. All was still. The songs of remembrance could only be heard in silence and only known in the hollow spaces of bone.

A shifting, gentle breeze moved through the clearing. It was not a breeze of time. It did not try to fasten itself to the memories of a shallow breath. Still, I felt traces of that breath reaching for me—the breath of tension, of push/pull, of action/reaction.

I knew that breath. It had ruled me once. But never had I felt how deeply it denied my Beauty.

It was the breath woven into the architecture of human striving—striving for significance in the eyes of others, for power drawn from feeding on static consciousness. But now, that breath could no longer command me.

I had touched Presence. I had breathed Radiance—unfolding from a space untouched by measured time. From this moment forward, meaning would no longer be grasped. It would be revealed. Not in tension. But in Presence.

A small bird landed nearby, tilting its head in curiosity. My whole being smiled. I didn't reach to name it or assign it meaning. Sacred offerings defy such definition. The bird simply reflected the song within the marrow of my hollow bones—a song I was only beginning to hear.

I remained there until the light began to shift into late afternoon. And when I rose, it was from an inner knowing that it was time. No questions. Only knowing. I stood slowly, my hand resting on a tree in silent gratitude. Nothing spoken. Nothing needed.

Each step back moved through layers of stillness, the ground anchoring the return of ancient memory awakening within the skeleton that now supported my movement. By the time I reached the cabin, a golden hush had descended across the forest.

Inside, the rays of light stretched through the windows, casting long bands across the wooden floor. I made tea without thought. My body remembered the movements. With the cup warm in my hands, I sat by the window, watching the outline of the forest dissolve into dusk.

I could still hear the echo of the words:
I call back the song of my bone marrow.

Not as a mantra. Not as a thought.
But as a hum that now moved with my breath,
with my silence, with my steps.

And I understood—without needing to name it:
I was not returning to ancient Truth.
I was becoming It.

Daily plans yielded to a rhythm that sang the harmonies of nature as my days took form. Tasks no longer pressed themselves forward but softened into invitations—moments of Presence rather than duties. Sometimes I rose with the dawn and sat beneath the porch's overhang, my skin drinking the gold-laced fog as it wrapped itself around me. Other mornings, I lingered beneath the quilt, breath syncing with the hush of snow on the roof, not yet ready to welcome spring's return.

Loneliness had no space here. The very air was filled with vibration—resonance of Beauty that surrounded and held me. Silence revealed its texture. Stillness pulsed its depth. And I began to realize how much of my life had been spent reacting to surfaces, to noise. Now, when the hum stirred, I didn't chase it with thought. I followed it with breath. With Presence.

One morning, as the scent of thawing Earth mingled with pine, I stood barefoot just beyond the porch, toes pressing into the softening soil. A light rain had fallen during the night, and now the forest exhaled a fragrance so ancient it bypassed memory entirely, entering me into a hollowing—sacred and timeless.

I walked into the trees without destination. The mind's planning was no longer needed. Each step carried its own pulse, harmonizing with the steady beat within me. In a small clearing—unadorned, subtle, almost invisible—I felt it before I saw it. Beauty, unshaped by time. Light filtering through branches fell in such a way that the ground itself seemed to curve inward, as though cradling something eternal.

I gasped, I stopped, I knelt.

There was no vision. No guiding voice. Only a deepening stillness.

And then, rising from marrow rather than thought, words I had always known:

You are the vessel and the Flame.

It was not metaphor. It was reality, resonant and undeniable.

I closed my eyes. The knowing settled where thought could not touch. Breath itself remembered for me. My mind had no part in it, and yet I knew.

I remained motionless. Not from effort, but because movement felt irrelevant. Presence—so vast it erased any edges of time or space—held me. I wasn't being shown. I wasn't being guided. I was being met. Met by the Self that had never been veiled, never been named, yet had always been here.

Silence unfurled into vastness. Space was no longer empty, but Presence Itself. Wholeness. Isness. Everywhere—beneath my skin, within the arch of branches, in the breath of Earth Itself.

Time dissolved. Minutes. Hours. A lifetime. None of it mattered.

When I finally arose, it was not "I" that stood. It was as though the stone released me, as naturally as a petal opening to sun. My movement was the forest's breath, Earth stepping itself through me. Gravity no longer weighed me—it became rhythm, softened into song.

By dusk, the sky wore the indigo that precedes true dark, and the first stars began to sing their tone into the night. I returned to the cabin, lit a single candle—not for light, but for witness. Its flame flickered gently, steadying my breath as I sat before it, palms open, empty.

You are the vessel and the Flame.

The words echoed—not in mind, but in marrow. And I understood: I was not waiting for the Divine to arrive.

I was Its arrival.

That night, the sky itself seemed to breathe. On its exhale, it widened above the cabin, spilling starlight across the clearing like embers of remembrance. I stood outside, my breath entwined with the subtle tide of the cool night air. No wind. No sound. Only the silent shimmer of constellations my bones had always remembered.

I lifted my gaze—not to the stars themselves, but to the vastness between them. The hollow of my bones longed for that space which asked nothing, proved nothing. It simply *was.* My blood sang with joy for the sight of this Presence—not because it came closer, but because I opened. My body received.

A chill touched my skin, and I did not flinch. The hum within me moved like a tide, echoing the earlier words—not as memory, but as living Truth:

You are the vessel and the Flame.

I closed my eyes. Earth's rhythm pulsed through my feet, through my breath, through the stillness of my form. And from deep within, I whispered:

I will remember. Even when I forget, I will remember.

The stars bore witness in silence. They did not answer. They did not need to. Their silence was acknowledgment.

And in the hush that followed, a smile rose without cause. My breath carried the quiet cadence of Radiance—each inhale drawing the night closer, each exhale letting it rest against my skin. Darkness did not press in; it opened outward, warm, seamless. In that seamlessness, I saw:

The night itself was the candle.

And I was its Flame.

Six

I awoke before dawn and lit the candle's low wick. Its faint flame melted into the wax as I replaced it with a new one. In that quiet beyond knowing, the candle revealed itself as the Flame—expanding, without moving, into all that seemed separate.

I understood now: I had not carried the Flame back into the forest. The forest had carried the Flame into me. Each breath was an exhale from the roots, each step a pulse from the mycelium beneath my feet. The stones remembered, the leaves remembered—and now my marrow remembered.

There was no "I" sending the Flame forward—only the Flame meeting Itself in new arrangements of wind, shadow, and heartbeat. When I walked, it was not my body crossing the ground—it was the Flame discovering another shape in which to shine.

Something in my mind stirred—a faint shadow of a threshold, as if an old sentinel stood watch. It asked nothing, yet I felt its quiet challenge. I didn't explain myself or push against it. I let the Flame expand until no space remained for questions. The sentinel didn't fall.

It faded, relieved. It had never guarded anything real—only a shadow it once believed in.

And there was no return. For the Flame had never left.

The quiet it left behind was not empty. It was full—of scent, of color, of the forest's nearness. I stepped outside. The air met me without crossing any boundary. Light pulsed through every detail—the glint on a fern, the slow turn of a leaf. None of it was outside of me; it was my awareness, moving through green and gold.

Far above, a raven called. Its cry deepened the silence.

The path opened ahead, leading back to my home. The scent of wood and smoke drifted toward me, carrying a welcome I had always known. Inside, the candle still burned, steady and unhurried.

I lowered into the chair—not to think or speak, but to let the Flame shape what came next. The wood beneath my hands radiated warmth, humming the same low chord that hummed through me. The walls softened into porous shapes, holding the air.

Nothing solid could name what I felt. I gave my bones to the hum of the chair. My breath no longer began or ended in the lungs—it moved without boundary.

A soft creak in the cabin; the settling of wood held an essence older than the walls, older than the forest that once gave them shelter.

And that movement was a moment of recognition—even the chair breathed the life that was breathing through me. The wood radiated the warmth of the day's sun, as my skin did, and its grain hummed the low chord moving through me. Resting my hands on my thighs, the weight of my palms lifted, as though they had been carrying something they could now set down.

The breath of the forest dissolved the lines of separation—between it, the room, and the chair supporting my pulsing bones. In the candle's still light, shadows curved across the table and the shelves, reflecting all that pulsed through the Flame.

Nothing solid, defined, or bound within limitation could name what I felt. To name it would be to step outside of it. I gave my bones to the hum of the chair. The breath I took neither began nor ended in my lungs.

My gaze came awake to receive the quiet without urgency. It was only the house exhaling—a structure accustomed to silence. Yet the resonance touched me. It carried an ancient essence of the forest that had filled this clearing long before the arms of time built the walls. My eyes rested on the candle's steady flame, its light wrapping gently around each shadow until the beginning and the ending of the flame merged.

My breath shifted—not deeper, not faster but with the faint sense of leaning forward into something unseen. In that awareness, I knew: the Flame would not always remain still. The knowing did not carry anticipation. It was not a promise of change, but the quiet weight of inevitability—like the scent of rain before the clouds gather. The Flame would inform me of what was next. It would move when It chose, and Its movement would carry me without force or explanation.

For now, I let the stillness cradle me, sensing the subtle currents beneath it—the way a tree, motionless in the air, is already turning light into life.

A faint quiver in the flame drew my gaze. It was not from a draft—the air was steady—but from something unmeasured, as if the light had felt my attention and responded. The shadow on the far wall swayed, slow and deliberate, like a tree in an unhurried wind that blew only to experience its own joy. I didn't lean forward. I surrendered my breath to its rhythm until it moved as my own. The moment held, unbroken, until I could no longer tell whether it was the shadow that swayed or the Flame Itself breathing through the room.

Somewhere beyond the walls, a branch snapped. Its muffled sound, softened by the moss that held its roots, passed through me without alarm and settled easily into the rhythm my still breath held. I turned my head slightly—not to seek the source, but to open to what had entered the moment. The air carried no change in scent, no shift in temperature, yet I knew the forest was nearer now. Perhaps it, too, had leaned in to listen.

My hands rested loosely in my lap, but my attention had already stepped beyond the door. I rose without deciding to rise. The chair released me easily, as though it, too, understood the rhythm drawing me forward. The candle flame wavered once—a gesture neither of farewell nor summons—and then steadied again. I stepped toward the door, my breath beating with the same unhurried measure as the shadow's sway on the wall.

When I opened it, the forest's cool breath met my skin. It did not greet me or call me; it simply continued beating its song, and I stepped into that song as though it had always been mine. The air outside felt neither cold nor warm. It was a space that held me, the way water holds a leaf. Shadows stretched long between the trees, not in retreat from the light, but as part of it.

My feet found the ground without thought. Each step, grounded within the Flame, arrived before it was even made. The path itself moved me forward. In the vastness above, a bird shifted on its branch.

The Crone's Flame: Radiance Made Flesh

The faint rustle folded into the greater stillness—a stillness my breath now inhabited.

Thoughts of where, how, why—they had no place in my motion. The Flame was walking; I was simply its vessel.

A shift in the air brushed my cheek, carrying none of the measured rhythm of wind—only a faint stirring, a space opening to receive me. The light among the trees thinned, revealing a thread of brightness winding deeper into the forest.

My steps followed the rhythm of my silent pulse within. The ground softened to hold each footprint, springing back as I passed. Water moved—a quick trickle over stone, its song so low I could not tell if it was near or far. I did not quicken my pace. What waited ahead was already in motion toward me, as certain as the breath that carried me forward.

The thread wove through the trees, neither straight nor winding—simply present, the way a river is present even when hidden beneath leaves. As I moved, it widened—not in size but in Presence—until the air itself felt lit from within. The scent reached me before the sight—fresh, mineral, carrying the cool depth of water drawn from stone. Then the glimmer broke through: a narrow stream, its surface catching the light like molten silver, moving with a quietness older than sound.

I stood at its edge, the Flame within me answering the Flame in the water. No boundary marked where one ended and the other began. The stream flowed, and I merged with its flow, as though we had been moving toward each other since before the forest was born.

The stream's song folded into the silence as naturally as breath into sleep. Everything stilled itself into a Presence where moments to count do not exist. I felt the water's shimmer thread through the marrow of my bones, loosening the stiffness in my joints. Without a cause, I turned from its edge. The path curved with the current, carrying its knowing into the forest. The Flame's Presence held each step, each breath, and I vowed to follow where It wished to go.

Behind me, the water kept flowing—unhurried, unchanged—its pulse lingering within me long after I left its light.

The days folded into one another with that same unhurried, unchanged rhythm as winter yielded to spring. I returned to the cabin often, not to escape the forest but to dwell in the seam where cabin and trees breathed as one. The wood stove ticked and sighed as I sat in its warmth, hands wrapped around a mug whose steam blurred the edges of thought.

Spring stirred at the edges of the forest. Buds flushed with the faint green of beginnings, their color pressing against the husk, almost ready to break into leaf. The air itself brightened, as if the season was inhaling before it spoke.

At night, I listened to the shifting timbers of the cabin, their creaks like the forest whispering through the walls. The Flame within me did not diminish in those hours; if anything, It deepened, pressing Its rhythm into the quiet marrow of my bones. The walks withdrew for a time, not gone but deepening in the hush, until they returned to me with the forest's summons.

Seven

The whisper of new leaves, ready to share their secrets, woke me at dawn. I rose into the softened light, the forest beckoning with a freshness that carried the scent of beginnings. Each breath drew me outward, into the trees where silence held both promise and mystery.

The path received me gently, its damp Earth carrying the imprint of night's cool breath. Branches arched low, stitching shadows across the path, their shifting patterns testing my step.

The Flame held steady in my chest, yet the air carried a faint density—a whisper from the mind's old territory. Thought stirred faintly, pressing to name this sensation, to prepare some defense. But the Flame expanded within me, dissolving the tension before it could gather.

A raven's shadow passed overhead—long and thin as the trees' own shadows—its wings stretched wide, announcing its presence. Its call did not come, but the wings beat with the rhythm of a deep drum, piercing the stillness.

The path curved. I could not see beyond it, yet in the bend the forest waited—certain I would have to step into its unseen depths before it revealed what lay ahead.

I stepped into the curve.

The air cooled, as if wishing to draw a thin veil across the forest's breath. My foot found the Earth, but each step grew heavier. Roots beneath the moss coiled faintly around my ankles in quiet question: "Are you certain?"

The Flame did not waver, but the mind stirred with familiar warnings, imagining shapes in the shadows and measuring the distance to them. Caution rose—not enough to turn me back, but enough to remind me of the comfort of boundaries.

Decision crept into my steps as the weight of the unseen pressed in. A single drop of water fell from a branch above, striking the ground with a sound too loud for its size. Its echo rattled the stillness as it traveled into the tangle of trunks and leaves.

Somewhere ahead, the light shifted—a faint golden pulse, as though the forest itself were breathing from a deeper center.

The pulse was not constant. It came as a slow wave, like sunlight bending through water. Each time it reached me, my ribs opened space to allow a fuller breath. Between those waves, the mind sought its foothold—measuring, recalling, warning, but the intervals between its thoughts stretched wider, soothing me like mist in sunlight.

I moved toward the light, not because I trusted it, but because an intuition older than trust recognized it. The ground softened, moss deepening to meet my steps. A scent, fresh and earthly, thickened the air, as if the forest had just turned over a page it had held for centuries.

High branches shifted without wind. Shafts of gold threaded through the canopy, meeting the path in broken pieces. I walked in

The Crone's Flame: Radiance Made Flesh

and out of that light as one might pass a threshold repeatedly without ever leaving the same room.

Somewhere within that pulsing light, a sound emerged—low, resonant, almost beneath hearing. It moved through the air as the deep notes of a drum move through bone. My breath caught its vibration.

The mind fell silent, not from surrender, but from losing its place in the rhythm.

The light thickened ahead, its golden thread weaving a doorway of such majesty it could not be bound by walls. No handle, no frame—just a threshold stitched from illumination itself.

I slowed, not from hesitation, but in knowing that this passage could not be crossed in haste. It asked reverence for its Beauty.

Each step was a deepening of grace, soaking through the marrow of my being as the resonance of the doorway merged with mine. Space warmed, fragrant with a sweetness I could not name. Remembrance carried its rains long vanished.

Leaves quivered in the scented breeze, greeting the return of the light. And in that moment, my knowing grew transparent: this Beauty was not light breaking into the forest. It was the forest revealing the light it always embodied.

I stood at the threshold, the golden seam before me breathing as though it, too, had been waiting. The mind—still lingering at the edge—reached for words, for meaning, for something to hold. But the Radiance allowed no foothold. It pressed gently into every thought until each one loosened and drifted apart, like petals falling from a flower gone to seed.

My surrender held no tones of giving up. It carried the tones of a love song—honoring what was, while giving to Beauty what Its essence could not touch. And through that love song, I stripped all that did not resonate with Beauty ... until the Flame within me and the light before me were no longer two presences. The duality of two dissolved into the Beauty that knows no separation.

The air enveloping me became weightless, though I had not moved. The seam of gold widened, not by opening, but by dissolving the sense that there had ever been a barrier. I felt the forest's breath as my own—no meeting, no parting, only flowing.

In that weightlessness, the Flame did not urge me forward. It radiated the illumined majesty of Its Beauty. I knew my step would never again be mine to take alone.

The seam of gold expanded until there was no longer a doorway, only the space that had been waiting behind it. Light and shadow folded into one another, not by blending but by exchanging places with a fluidity that defied the mind's need for sequence.

I stepped forward without the sense of crossing anything. The forest around me did not shift; it revealed. Every trunk, every leaf, every ripple of air seemed to breathe from a shared, central pulse.

A shape emerged ahead—not apart from the trees, but woven from them. The lines of its form were both branch and wing, its surface both bark and scale. The dragon stood in stillness, Its eyes deep as the soil's oldest memory.

Its breath rose and fell with mine. No fire leapt from its mouth—the Flame was already here, with us both, beyond our separated forms. It did not summon me forward nor hold me back; It simply existed as the perfect mirror of my own wholeness.

The Crone's Flame: Radiance Made Flesh

When I inhaled, I felt the breath of its wings stretching into the unseen. When I exhaled, the warmth of its breath wrapped through the marrow of my bones.

The Flame within me answered—not in words, but in the slow, steady rhythm of integration. There was no union to be achieved, for we had never been two. The dragon's gaze was the gaze of my own soul meeting itself without the fog of forgetting.

And in that gaze, the forest fell utterly silent.

The silence did not press; it expanded. It moved into every hollow place, filling it not with sound but with the Presence of nothing lacking. My body felt the weight of its own release—a gravity of letting go.

The dragon's breath deepened once, twice, and with each breath, the shimmer of Its form began to loosen back into the trees. There was no ending—only the dispersal of a shape reminding me of what I had always carried within.

I stood alone, yet not alone. Every thread of the forest's light, every shadow across the moss, every sigh of the air was the dragon's breath now moving through me.

And as I turned to walk deeper into the unseen, the Flame walked with me, as Me.

The Crone's Flame of Isness:
The Dragon's Breath of Eternal Presence

I am the breath before the first word,
the hush that gives birth to Flame and river alike.
I am the seam of gold unbroken,
the silence expanding without edge or end.

I do not arrive, nor do I depart,
I remain, moving only as the joy of my own Being.
I am the Flame that drinks the Water,
the Water that kindles the Flame.

The Crone's Flame: Radiance Made Flesh

I am the dragon's breath upon your marrow,
the wingbeat stirring memory in the soil.
I am the gaze that looks through Itself
and finds only Beauty, sovereign and whole.

Do not seek me at thresholds or ending

Eight

On a day flushed with spring's warmth and sunlight, my daughter arrived, carrying the bright hum of everyday life. She brought stories from town, her laughter scattering through the cabin like quick birds startled into flight. I listened, smiling, letting the warmth of her presence fill spaces the forest could not reach.

Yet I noticed differences in the way I now received her. Her words felt heavier than before, thick with the weight of things that no longer clung to me. The brightness she carried was edged with urgency, as if the world she came from pressed against her shoulders, urging me to return with her.

At moments, when our eyes met, I felt both the closeness of blood and the distance of worlds. She studied me with quiet unease, as though searching for the mother she remembered and finding instead a silence she could not name. Between us hung a fragrance—not of disease, but of unfamiliarity, like the air before a storm.

Her hand found mine. "Mom, you can't keep living like this. Alone, out here … it isn't healthy. You need people, normal life. You need to come back."

Her voice trembled, not with anger but with fear—fear of losing me, fear of what she could not understand.

I let the silence breathe between us, then drew her into an embrace. My arms wrapped around her not as a shield nor comfort alone, but as the Radiance of Presence that needed no conditions. She leaned into me—but only for a moment.

When she pulled back, her eyes searched mine, brimming with hesitation. "I just don't want to lose you."

I smiled, not with assurance she could measure, but with the clarity of being that asked for no promise. "You cannot lose me—I am here, always, in the way Love remembers."

She studied me for a long moment, unease still lingering, then kissed my cheek and stepped toward the door. At the threshold, she turned once more. "Promise me you'll be all right?"

"I already am."

She nodded, though the answer did not reach her. With a final glance, she slipped outside, her presence folding into the rhythm of the forest.

The cabin's silence expanded, not empty but full, as though the trees themselves had moved closer to steady the space she left behind. The Flame within me glowed brighter, gathering even her concern into Its quiet pulse of remembrance.

I lingered in the cabin after she left, the silence swelling around me like a tide. Yet the forest called again, its pull deepened by the dragon's lingering Presence. I answered its call.

The Crone's Flame: Radiance Made Flesh

The path opened before me, damp with spring's breath, as if the Earth itself had been waiting. Each step carried me deeper into its embrace, the hush of branches above echoing the steady hum within my chest. Shadows pooled beneath the arching trees, their patterns bending to mark a passage.

The air thickened with mist, cool against my skin. At the forest's heart, a hollow revealed itself, where water gathered into a darkened pool. The surface trembled, as though stirred from below. A vibration, steady and resonant, threaded into my marrow. My inner Flame answered, not with fear but recognition—an ancient rhythm echoing through my bones.

And then the dragon's Presence rose—vast, deliberate, undeniable. A shimmer moved through my depths, older than memory, breaking water, breaking silence. Breath yielded of itself, until nothing remained to give or to take. Presence moved as gaze, as song—no witness, no singer, only Radiance beholding Itself.

I had long believed Beauty must be held close, protected from the world's shadows, as if Its Radiance could be tainted. But in the yielding, I saw the truth: Beauty, Wisdom, Love—none of these were shields. They were not fragile treasures to be hidden away: they were the very substance of existence.

The tension I carried, the subtle strain of holding Radiance against intrusion, dissolved. And in its dissolving, I felt the release of a burden I had never named. I breathed and Beauty breathed me. I opened, and Radiance was everywhere—untouched by the muck I once feared.

In that clarity, even the muck shimmered, revealed as never separate from the Flame Itself.

And the dragon's whisper curled through me like breath upon embers:

What if the muck you fled was never impurity at all, but Radiance in disguise? What if the shield you carried—so heavy, so wearying—was the only veil that kept you from seeing it shimmer?

Lay it down, Julia. Just for a breath. Do not defend Beauty for it cannot be harmed. Do not guard Radiance, for It cannot be dimmed. Let the shield slip from your hands and notice what remains. You may find that what you once called shadow was already the light, waiting for you to stop fighting.

The dragon's voice faded, yet Its echo did not. It resounded through the hollow of my bones, sharper than thought, deeper than breath. I could not turn away. The shield was no longer in my hands; it had never been.

The muck shimmered before me, unmasked, neither to be feared nor transmuted. Radiance was already there, gleaming through every thread of shadow.

In the stillness that followed, I felt no need to answer, no need to reach. Presence gazed, Presence sang—and I dissolved within Its echo.

Around me, the forest breathed differently. Branches no longer arched as shadows to be tested, but as living arches of Radiance. The ground, damp with moss and decay, shimmered as though lit from within, every fallen leaf a vessel of Presence. Even the air moved with quiet recognition, carrying the dragon's echo in its stillness.

What now seemed as barrier opened as invitation. The world was not against me, nor even beside me. It was the same Radiance I had tried to shield, revealed everywhere, in everything.

Each step forward no longer felt like passage through a forest but like walking deeper into Radiance Itself. The path was not a way through—it was a way in. The Flame within my chest no longer led me; It was the ground beneath me, the air around me, the pulse through every root and stone.

I was not moving through the world. The world was moving through me—no longer outside but within, around, and as Me.

The path stretched on, yet it no longer felt like a way forward. Each step was not a journey but a deepening—the forest, the air, the very soil dissolving into the same Radiance now pulsing through my marrow. The horizon was not ahead of me; it was within me, unfolding with every breath.

The Flame within no longer guided me as something apart. It was the pulse of the ground beneath my feet, the breath of branches swaying overhead, the quiet shimmer of moss and stone. I could not tell where my body ended and the world began, nor did I need to.

There was only Radiance walking Itself.

The horizon within me swelled—not a line of distance but an opening without end. Each breath widened it further, until the very notion of "ahead" dissolved. The forest no longer held me; it flowed as Me.

Somewhere in that vastness, the dragon's Presence lingered—not as a figure to follow, but as the rhythm of my marrow, as the silent fire threading through Earth and sky. I was no longer seeking It. I was no longer yielding to It. I was It.

The forest bowed in quiet recognition. Light spilled through the canopy, not as sun filtering through leaves, but as Radiance unveiling Itself in every particle of air. The pool at the hollow's heart no longer mirrored the world above it—it shimmered as if its depths and the sky had become one expanse.

Even the silence changed. It was no longer absence of sound, but the fullness of Presence, carrying the pulse of Earth, the breath of wind, the hush of waters. Nothing moved, yet everything was moving—through me, with me, as Me.

The path did not end, yet it no longer mattered whether I walked or stood still. Each moment was the same vastness, the same unfolding. The dragon's echo was not behind me, nor ahead of me—It was within every pulse, every shimmer of leaf and stone.

In that completeness, I knew: nothing could be lost, nothing could be found. Radiance had never departed, and It could never fade.

The stillness lingered, yet the forest stirred with a gentler rhythm. My steps resumed, not to seek, not to arrive, but as the simple play of Presence through form. Each sound—the hush of water over stone, the creak of branches swaying—was part of the same Radiance that breathed me.

The dragon no longer rose as figure or echo; It threaded through the marrow of the Earth, through the sky's vast silence, through the hollow of my own bones.

The forest pressed with no mystery. It opened as familiar, every root and branch woven with the same rhythm that moved through me. Even the mist that once veiled the path seemed less like concealment and more like the breath exhaled by the Earth.

I walked without effort, without destination. The path beneath me was not guiding, nor was I following. There was only the quiet play of Radiance moving in form—each step a pulse, each breath a gleam of the same song.

The Crone's Flame: Radiance Made Flesh

And in that ordinariness, I felt a deeper wonder than before. Radiance no longer thundered as revelation or blazed as Presence—It simply was. The extraordinary had folded itself into the ordinary, and I into it.

The air moved with a softer cadence, carrying not portent but ease. Birdsong, once sharp against the silence, now blended as if it had always been part of the same breath. Even the smallest stirrings—the ripple of water against stone, the shift of light on bark—were woven into the same seamless Presence.

There was nothing to guard against, nothing to seek. The path was not a trial, nor a revelation, but the simple unfolding of Radiance in form. Each step was whole in itself, untouched by past or promise.

From the corner of my sight, the pool at the hollow's edge began to glow. Its surface no longer reflected what was above but seemed lit from within, as though light was rising from its depths. The forest leaned into the glow, every branch and stone stilled in quiet witness.

The water did not ripple. It opened—darkness giving way to Radiance, Its depths lifting into form. My breath moved with It, not from effort but from recognition—something known, yet not remembered, was pressing forward.

Within the glow, a contour began to rise—not of scale or wing, not of bone or flesh, but of Presence leaning into form. It was a voice before It was a figure, a resonance gathering Itself into sound.

The pool shimmered, and what rose from its depths was not separate from me, yet not confined to me. It was Radiance, choosing a new face, a new way to be heard.

The quiet deepened, holding me in its breathless embrace.

Nothing more was needed—the Radiance had already spoken in the peace, and I was Its echo.

Nine

Morning light seeped through the cabin's shutters, soft and unhurried. I awoke feeling immense peace, as if arising from a depth older than the night itself. The forest moved through the walls and through me; its rhythm no longer separate, but the same rhythm as my own pulse.

The dragon's Presence breathed within, not as something approaching but as the quiet shimmer of Radiance woven into the ordinary. The fire in the hearth had burned down to embers, their glow carrying the same song that had once held me in the hollow's depths.

I rose in rhythm with the pulse, not to begin my day, but to move within what had never ceased. The air greeted me as I stepped outside, cool and companionable. Dew jeweled the grass, birds stitched their calls into the morning, and the stream—swollen from the heavy rains—sang with unrestrained abundance.

Kneeling at its edge, I touched the water. Its cold surge and my warm blood now moved as one. There was a time such moments felt fragile, as if Beauty could vanish when I looked away. Now it lingered, steady, unbound by my attention. Presence was already whole, needing nothing to be complete.

And yet, as I lifted my hand from the stream, a faint unease stirred. Not danger, not absence—only reminder that Radiance was not yet finished with me.

Leaves, bright with spring, swayed with quiet assurance. Their green sang the song of Presence; the air carried the scent of damp soil and budding blossoms. Each fragrance was a thread in the same weave that pulsed within my chest.

I returned to the cabin, letting the day unfold in its small rhythm—tending the fire, preparing food, moving in the simplicity of living. Each gesture shimmered in its wholeness, complete as it was. By evening, I felt the call to rest, as though even my body knew more was to come.

Night gathered. The hearth's glow softened into silence, and I yielded to sleep with the sense of something waiting beyond the veil.

Morning returned with a gentleness, reluctant to wake me. Light slipped through the shutters, softer than before, as though the forest itself wished to linger in stillness a little longer.

I moved slowly, as though each gesture needed to honor the quiet. The embers in the hearth glowed faintly; I stirred them, not to summon the flame, but to keep their warmth alive. Breakfast was simple, each bite steadying me in the ordinary, anchoring me in the world of touch and breath before stepping into what lay ahead.

Yet as I prepared the meal, the mind stirred, trying to take charge—directing even the I Am, as though Presence needed its orders. It played its small games, pretending to control what was never its own. I watched, amused, as even those whispers dissolved into the greater Flame. Presence required no director; It moved through the stirring, the lifting, the tasting, whole unto Itself.

And in that dissolving, the contrast became clear. Where once the mind ruled with its hard edges, now there was only the gentleness of Presence—flowing, unforced, quietly loving. Tears rose, not from grief, but as a tribute to the long difficulty of living under the mind's dominion. The weeping was not sorrow, but relief, as if even my marrow bowed in gratitude for the ease of this unfolding.

When I finally opened the cabin door, the air was different. Not brighter, not heavier, but charged—as if the forest had been waiting for this moment. The trees stood with quiet expectancy, their leaves catching the early light in translucent green. The stream's voice had softened, its song less urgent, more like a beckoning murmur.

I followed the invitation without thought of destination. My steps surrendered to the forest's rhythm until the path curved toward a clearing, a hush already gathering there. The light was unlike sunlight—clearer, more translucent, as though Radiance had chosen this place to pause Its own reflection.

The clearing opened with a light not of the sun. It shimmered, not above or around, but from within everything—air, branch, stone, soil. It was as though Radiance had chosen this place to reveal Itself more nakedly, unshielded by form.

The light here was not illumination—it was unveiling. Every leaf, every stone seemed to shine with a pulse that was both within and beyond itself, as though the clearing were remembering Its own depth.

Around me, the hush deepened. Each leaf listened, its stillness more eloquent than sound. A shimmer rose, not from the sky above, but from the ground beneath—light welling up through soil and stone until the air itself quivered with translucence.

The Flame in my chest answered, widening, steadying. There was no boundary between Its pulse and the clearing's glow; it was one current unfolding through different faces.

I stood within it, not apart, every breath both mine and not mine. The Presence did not arrive from elsewhere. It unveiled Itself from within and around, like Beauty remembering Its own name.

The shimmer gathered, condensing into a Radiance that breathed with me. Outside and within merged into one—permeating marrow and soil, sky and silence.

A current moved through the clearing as a living tide of Presence that was not of wind nor of water. It pressed through me gently, insistently, until the boundaries that once defined me dissolved into Its flow.

No vision appeared, no voice spoke. And yet the recognition was undeniable. It was the same pulse I had felt in the hollow, the same song that had steadied me in the cabin—now magnified, unveiled, impossible to turn away.

The current thickened, not with weight, but with density of Presence—like air so saturated with light it turned to substance. My body did not resist; it yielded as though it had always known this tide. The marrow of my bones hummed, each vertebra a string tuned to the same note the forest carried. My breath dissolved into the greater Breath, a rhythm that asked nothing and yet consumed all illusion of apartness.

Thought stirred—fragile, a ripple breaking the surface of a vast lake. It did not hold, could not hold. Even thought bowed, folding back into stillness, vanishing in the gaze of what has no border.

The Crone's Flame: Radiance Made Flesh

At the heart of the stillness, something stirred—a movement without motion, a voice without sound. It was the voice of the marrow itself speaking, older than thought, older than form.

The Flame widened, leaning into the call, steadying for revelation. This was no echo of Presence—It was Presence as my very substance. A knowing without words, a song without melody, pressed against the threshold of flesh. Recognition trembled through me: this unveiling would not pass.

The Presence pressed closer, opening into a rising spiral as though the marrow itself had decided to speak. Its nearness was not external; it welled from within, filling the spaces where thought once lingered.

The forest did not vanish, nor did I leave myself behind. Instead, both opened—each branch, each breath, each cell of my being—until all pulsed as one undivided field.

Recognition required embodiment—flesh itself had to carry it. It was not enough to feel or know. It insisted on being lived, breathed, walked.

The Flame expanded as a resonance, Its current spiraling outward and inward at once. Every thread of marrow, every filament of breath, joined the widening pulse. The forest did not surround me—it was unified with the same expansion, spiraling through leaf, stream, and stone, no part standing outside the unfolding.

Presence would not remain a shimmer in awareness. It demanded embodiment—the living pulse of flesh and Earth. The spiral carried me further, each turn dissolving the husk of separation until even the word "within" no longer applied.

A recognition coursed through me—a tremor of my marrow's certainty of its own song. Every thread of Radiance long buried in flesh rose to the surface, revealing what had never been hidden.

I was not beholding Presence. Presence was beholding Itself through me. And in that beholding, nothing of the old scaffolding of self remained.

This is not arrival.

This is remembrance made flesh.

There was no center, no circumference, only the ease of belonging. I did not dissolve into vastness—I was unveiled as vastness embodied.

What had once felt like a Presence entering now unveiled as what had always been my marrow, my breath, my gaze. Radiance did not arrive; it unveiled Itself as the one who had been waiting.

In that unveiling, a vow formed—not of effort or promise, but of inevitability. Flesh itself whispered it, bone carried it, blood sang it: never again would I pretend to be less than I Am.

The vow was not spoken to heaven nor Earth, but to the Flame that is Both. It needed no words, yet its certainty resounded:

I Am Radiance made flesh.

The vow did not end in silence—it ignited movement. Each Breath seemed to walk Itself, each step to consecrate the ground. I was no longer carrying Radiance into the world; Radiance was carrying me.

The Flame did not burn as a private fire but as the pulse of creation itself, widening through bone and sky alike. Its current pressed outward and inward at once, revealing every fiber of existence as holy.

I realized then that to live was not to hold Radiance but to let It hold me, unceasing, unshakeable. Nothing needed to be remembered, for remembrance had already become flesh.

Even the air shimmered as if relieved of its task to separate. Breath moved freely as exchange, each inhalation already answered, each exhalation already received. There was no giver, no receiver—only the seamless circulation of Radiance through all.

In that circulation, joy rose—not as emotion, but as natural Radiance of being unbound. It did not swell or fade; It simply was, steady as the marrow's pulse.

I walked, though I was not walking. I breathed, though I was not breathing. Life was not mine to carry. Life was carrying Itself through me, as Me.

And so it was: the Flame no longer within, but everywhere—Earth, sky, silence and song, flesh and marrow—Radiance beholding Radiance, unending.

Ten

The days did not return to what they had been. Even the simplest gesture—lifting a cup, stepping across the threshold, touching the wooden table—carried the same inevitability as Breath. Nothing began, nothing ended. Each act moved as Radiance made visible.

Silence was no absence; it was the pulse beneath sound. The cry of a hawk, the murmur of water, the crack of firewood—all were variations of one seamless song. There was no need to remember Presence; the marrow itself could no longer forget.

And yet, ease carried its own demand. Embodiment was not the bliss of dissolving into light—it was the insistence of living it among the textures of form. Hunger still arose. Wood still had to be split. The body still ached with its old patterns. Radiance did not erase these; It filled them with the unmistakable shine of Its Presence.

There were moments of dissonance. The body leaned toward habit, toward the memory of scarcity, toward the reflex to guard itself. In those moments, Presence did not vanish but pressed closer, requiring choice. I felt It asking, "Will you stay open when the old pulse whispers otherwise?"

It was then I understood: revelation had been the threshold, not the completion. Radiance would not remain as a shimmer in the marrow if It did not flow into relation—into how I touched wood, how I tasted water, how I met another's gaze.

I began to see that Radiance was not tested in moments of stillness, but in movement. To split wood without resentment, to wash dishes without hurry, to walk a worn path without drifting into absence—these were the altars where Presence proved Itself embodied.

The mind sometimes whispered, "Surely the greater moments have passed. Surely the revelation is behind you." But Radiance pressed back with a quieter Truth: "This, too, is holy. This, too, is where I live."

It was not about escaping the weight of flesh but letting flesh itself shine. Pain did not always vanish, but it no longer carried exile. Fatigue still came, but it did not sever me from the pulse. Even in frailty, Radiance moved unbroken.

I realized then that wholeness was not measured by the absence of fracture, but by the Presence that moved even through the cracks. Radiance was not fragile. It needed no protection. It entered every gap, every silence, every broken edge, filling them until even imperfection became holy ground.

The seasons themselves seemed to move differently now. Spring was not a promise of what would come, autumn not a loss of what had been. Each turn of Earth unfolded as immediacy. The sap rising in the trees, the frost silvering the grass, the long hush of winter nights—all were variations of the same unbroken Presence.

Yet I also saw how easily the old habits tried to return. The mind longed for progress, for a summit beyond the horizon. The body leaned toward familiar ache, toward the caution of conserving itself. But Presence was patient, pressing not with command but with quiet constancy. It was never elsewhere, never withheld, only waiting for my willingness to meet It again.

The days gathered themselves into a different rhythm, not marked by striving, but by the quiet continuity of being met anew. Tasks once noticed became thresholds. Lifting water, sweeping the floor, mending a tear in cloth—each offered the chance to meet Presence or to fall back into absence. Even in absence, Radiance did not withdraw. It lingered, patient, until I remembered again.

I began to see how easily the mind wanted to divide: sacred here, mundane there; depth in stillness, distraction in movement. But Radiance dissolved such borders with a single gesture. A bird taking flight was no less holy than the hush before dawn. The ache in my hands after splitting wood bore the same shimmer as the stars. Nothing was excluded; everything belonged.

Even memory shifted. What once felt like a past to measure or escape revealed itself as another pulse of Presence, not behind me but within me. Regret loosened its grip; longing softened. It was not that the past was erased, but that it no longer claimed authority over the now. Radiance infused even memory, making it porous, transparent to the greater song.

In this new rhythm where Radiance infused Its Presence into ordinary life, choice remained. Not as effort, but as willingness—again and again—to let each moment reveal what had always been. The path was not to ascend beyond the ordinary, but to walk it until even the ordinary unveiled itself as holy ground.

The ordinary became a kind of teacher. Its lessons did not come as proclamations, but as quiet insistence. To listen when impatience rose, to stay present when loneliness whispered, to soften where anger bristled—each moment invited me deeper into embodiment.

I began to see that Radiance was not waiting at the end of a path, but already here, pressing close in the smallest gestures. A smile given and received, the weight of a log carried from the pile, the warmth of bread in my hands—each bore the same current as great revelations.

Yet as Beauty sang through the ordinary, It made space for my faltering. Even forgetting was held within Presence. Radiance was never diminished by my absence; It waited for my willingness to return.

Through the gentleness of quiet grace breathing through the ordinary, I understood that nothing needed to be extraordinary to be holy. The taste of water on my tongue, the creak of the cabin's wood as it settled into the night, the way shadows lengthened across the floor—all revealed themselves as doorways opened to me. Presence was not hidden behind them but alive within them, asking only that I pause long enough to notice.

Sometimes, I found myself reaching back toward the memory of revelation, longing to feel again the immensity of the clearing or the marrow's song. But even that longing became transparent. It was not Radiance I was missing, only the drama of Its unveiling. Radiance was here, steady, unshaken by whether I noticed or not. The Flame had already become flesh; It no longer required spectacle to prove Itself.

There were moments when the ache of the body spoke louder than stillness—shoulders stiff after work, breath shallow with fatigue. Yet even these did not stand outside Presence. The ache itself shimmered when I yielded to it, revealing not an enemy to resist, but a rhythm asking to be met. Radiance did not wait for perfection of form. It pressed through every crack and weakness, shining all the more clearly because of them.

My clarity expanded, now seeing that embodiment was less about holding on to Radiance and more about letting Radiance hold me. When I allowed Radiance to cradle me, there was no effort to maintain, no vigilance required. Breath carried It. Pulse carried It. Even silence carried It. The work did not ask me to rise above it, but to dwell fully within it. Until nothing remained outside of the circle of holiness.

The ease of solitude could not shield me forever. Inevitably, the world pressed close again. A neighbor stopped by with casual words about weather and work, yet beneath them lingered the unspoken weight of expectation: Was I useful? Did I belong? Old reflexes stirred—the urge to justify, to present myself as worthy.

Doubt whispered, as it always had: "What if they cannot see you? What if your silence is mistaken for lack?" Fear hovered near, carrying the memory of being measured, diminished, overlooked. My chest tightened, the old pulse of defense quickening.

But even as the body braced, Radiance did not recede. It pressed closer, steady as Breath, Its Love melting the conquering impulse of the mind. This mind was learning to speak with a new voice that carried the current of Presence. And when it felt doubt, fear, the urge to prove—it allowed Presence to hold them without collapse.

Culture's demands and the mind's fears carried the same current of force that echoed the same pattern: the forgetting of Radiance. Each time they arose, they became thresholds, not barriers. To meet another's gaze without shrinking, to allow silence without apology, to let my worth shine without defense—these became acts of remembrance.

The old voices did not vanish overnight. They returned, sometimes fierce, sometimes subtle. Yet with each return, Radiance revealed Its patience. Doubt no longer meant absence of Presence; it became another doorway to step through, another chance to let Radiance live through me.

The voices of culture arrived through more than neighbors or news: they rose within me as archetypal echoes—ancient, persistent. One voice whispered of scarcity, insisting I must earn my right to be here. Another murmured of comparison, forever measuring my worth against unseen scales. A harsher one carried the blade of shame, reminding me of where I had faltered. They spoke in the accents of memory, yet their weight was older than my own life, threads woven through generations.

These voices—they lost their force when they met the rhythm of Radiance, slowly mellowing their growl. The neighbor's casual glance lost its sense of judgment as it began to mirror my own doubt. The silence when conversation ended no longer demanded a filler. Even shame, when it stirred, revealed itself as a veil stretched over the same Presence. My deepened vision now saw culture's loudest demands, and the mind's deepest fears, not as enemies but disguises—thin garments covering what had never been diminished.

The Crone's Flame: Radiance Made Flesh

As much as I wanted to avoid the world, I knew that I had to find the strength to remain transparent within it. To let its demands pass through me without carving their weight into my marrow. To stand amid noise without losing the song beneath it. This was not withdrawal, but a deeper engagement—the courage to remain porous, so that nothing was kept outside of Presence.

It was with thoughts of my daughter that Presence pressed most deeply. Time had passed since we had last been together, and in that distance lay a quiet ache. The last time I saw her at the cabin, there was worry in her eyes about the woman I was becoming and the life I was choosing. We grew distant since then. I wondered how she now saw me—would her eyes still search for the mother she remembered and wanted me to be?

The old pulse stirred quickly here: guilt for the times I had not been enough, doubt over whether absence had left scars. Yet even as those voices rose, Radiance did not waver. It asked me gently: *Will you let her meet who you are now, without apology for who you were?*

A golden thread of Presence wove Itself within our bond that I once thought was only of blood and memory. Each time I imagined her face, I felt Radiance move—not as judgment, but as invitation. The relationship was not a ledger of rights and wrongs; it was another field where embodiment would be tested, where Presence would be asked to live in the most human of exchanges: listening, forgiving, receiving, and being received.

I did not know what words would be spoken when we met again. Perhaps they would be awkward, perhaps tender. Perhaps silence would carry more than sentences. But I knew this: I could not return to her with the armor of the past. Only with the marrow's song alive in me, trusting that even in the knots of family, Radiance was already waiting.

Eleven

The path back to Linda carried a weight unlike the forest's silence. The weight was not of dread, but of threads woven long by choice. This body remembered the rhythm of Linda's footsteps in the cabin, the curve of her questions, the worry in her gaze. The time that had passed since then was not a clean break; it was a quiet widening of distance.

A brew of concerns—old reflexes stirring—accompanied me as I drove to Linda's. The concerns I had before now wore a certain charge that wanted to break through my peace: "Would she recognize me as I am now, or would she search for the mother she once knew?" The questions pressed at the marrow, asking whether Radiance could breathe as fully in family as It did in solitude.

The chorus of old voices grew with each mile, the sense of distance that had dissolved in the forest returning as I neared Linda's house.

When I reached Linda's door, my hand hesitated before knocking. Not from fear of rejection, but from the knowing that this moment was more than reunion. It was a mirror, a test of embodiment. *Could*

I stand here without armor, without apology, letting Radiance meet her gaze through mine?

Linda opened the door before I could knock, and I knew she had been waiting. She, too, felt the uneasiness of change. Her eyes searched mine quickly, the instinctive scan of a daughter measuring what had changed.

For a heartbeat, silence stood between us. I felt the urge to fill it—explain myself, reassure her, bridge the time of absence with words. But Radiance steadied me with Its remembrance: silence was invitation.

"Hi, Mom," she said at last, her voice carrying both relief and hesitation.

"Linda," I answered simply, and in that simplicity something softened.

She stepped aside, gesturing me in. The house smelled of bread and coffee, alive with the textures of a life carried forward. Photographs lined the walls, small altars of memory. I saw myself in some of them—moments I had nearly forgotten, now fixed in her keeping.

We sat, and at first our words were small, polite, circling the edges: how the cabin fared, the weather, the seasons passing. Yet beneath each sentence was another current. Stronger, unspoken. The old ache tugged at me—"Will she think me careless, absent, selfish?" But then her hand brushed mine, light as breath.

"I was worried about you," she said. No accusation, just truth.

"I know," I whispered. The marrow's song rose within me to hold this moment as holy ground—silencing the mind's urge to defend and justify.

Her eyes glistened, though she looked away quickly. "You seem ... different. Lighter, maybe. But also further away."

I breathed, letting her words pass through me rather than cling. "I'm here now," I said.

And for the first time her gaze rested in mine without searching. Not complete, not resolved, but open.

For a while we stayed like that, her gaze in mine, neither of us speaking. I felt the gulf between us—wide, silent, impossible to fill with words. In that stillness, I understood: no story of mine could close the distance. What she longed for was not explanation but the reassurance of Presence.

So I did not explain. I did not rush to bridge the silence. Instead, I let my breath slow, let my eyes soften, and allowed the marrow's song to steady me. Who she met in that moment was not the mother she remembered, but the Presence that carried us both.

She shifted slightly, unsettled by what she could not name. "Sometimes," she said, voice low, "I don't know who you are anymore."

Her words held no malice, only bewilderment. I let their nuance move through me like wind through leaves. "I know," I said gently. "And I can't be who I was. But I am here."

The weight of her shoulders loosened a little. She looked down at her hands, turning her cup as though its warmth might steady her. "I don't understand this path you've chosen. It feels … far away from me."

I leaned closer—closer into the remembrance my flesh now breathed through, and closer to her within this Presence. "You don't have to understand," I whispered. "Only know that the love between us hasn't gone anywhere."

Something softened in her then. Not resolution, not comprehension—but a loosening in her breath. She nodded, almost imperceptibly, and in that small gesture, the void between us thinned enough to hold a fragile peace.

We lingered in that quiet, neither forcing the moment into more than it could hold. The gulf between us had not closed, but it had softened enough to breathe. Presence did not demand that we understand each other, only that we honor the space between us, free of judgment.

She poured more coffee, her movements steadying her. Her hands moved through the strength and familiarity of carrying the weight of a life lived in rhythm with work, family, and obligation. Those hands had once cradled me in the ways of love I once knew, just as mine once cradled her. Now, as her hands turned her cup slowly, they searched for ground. She sensed that foothold of love no longer present as it once was.

"Do you ever get lonely?" she asked suddenly, her eyes not meeting mine.

Her question carried more than curiosity. It held her own fear—that solitude was emptiness, that distance meant abandonment.

"I used to," I said. "But it's different now. Solitude doesn't feel empty. It feels … full. It's not the absence of Love—it's where I found It."

Her brow furrowed, trying to bridge the words to her own experience. For her, love had always been tethered to doing, to proving, to Presence made visible through service. What I spoke of was a Love without anchor, without proof, a Love she could not yet touch.

And yet, she listened. She did not push back, did not laugh, did not dismiss. That, too, was a threshold: her willingness to hear without closing the door.

Linda's silence lingered after my words; a silence that held the gentleness of wondering. She stared past me for a moment, as if trying to place this new Presence she sensed into the frame of the mother she once knew. The frame no longer fit, and we both felt that misfit.

I followed her glance at the photographs on the wall—moments captured and preserved, each holding an image of me she still longed to recognize. Birthdays, holidays, the easy laughter of years when my role was clear. Those images seemed to ask, "Why could you not remain here?

"Why did you have to become someone else?"

"I don't know how to reach you anymore," she said softly, her hand resting on the table as if steadying herself.

The ache of her words pressed close, yet I did not collapse into them. Radiance steadied me. "You don't have to reach me," I said gently. "I'm not apart from you. Even if I look different, what matters between us hasn't gone anywhere."

Her lips pressed tight, caught between wanting to believe and fearing it was not true. She shook her head slightly. "It doesn't feel that way. It feels like you chose something that left us behind." For a moment, the weight of her grief rose into me, stirring the mind's familiar impulse to justify, to explain. But the marrow's song steadied me again. Inwardly, the vow whispered itself through me—not as words I offered her, but as the truth I could not leave behind:

I Am Radiance made flesh.

"I didn't leave Love behind," I whispered. "I left the stories that kept me from knowing It fully. That Love—It's still here, between us, whether you feel It or not."

Her shoulders eased a little, not with full understanding, but with the faint shift of breath when the burden grows lighter.

She sat back, folding her arms as though to guard the ache that had surfaced. Her gaze softened, though, almost against her will. "Maybe I don't know how to love you like this," she admitted. The words trembled as they left her, unshielded, as if they cost her something to speak aloud.

I felt the sting of them, not as a wound, but as truth revealed. "This is the void," I thought. It was the void of Linda's bewilderment—her love meeting a Love she could not recognize.

"You don't have to know how," I said softly. "Just being here, listening, is enough. Love doesn't need us to understand It—It asks that we allow It."

Her arms loosened, and she exhaled as though something unclenched within her. A silence followed, this time not heavy, but tentative, like a door slightly open.

"I don't want to lose you," she whispered.

"You won't," I said steady and quiet, letting the marrow's song carry the truth of it. "I'm not lost. I'm here. Maybe not in the way you expected—but I am here."

For the first time, her eyes filled, and she did not look away.

We sat in that fragile openness, neither of us reaching to mend it, neither turning away. It was not resolution, but it was something—two hearts recognizing each other within the depths that each could carry.

I felt the vow move within me again, not as words I spoke, but as marrow's steadiness to remain here without collapsing, without hiding, without apology. To let Love stand where explanation could not.

Linda brushed at her eyes quickly, embarrassed by their wetness. "I'm not sure I know how to be with you anymore," she admitted in a whisper.

"You don't have to know," I said gently. "We'll find our way together. It doesn't need to be the same as before—it can't be the same as before."

Her lips trembled at my words, the ache still there, but softened. She nodded once, and in that small nod I felt the tiniest thread woven back into place—not the old bond, not the old certainty, but a thread that could hold us in the now.

The room held a different kind of silence now—less of an unknown void, more of a shared ground that could breathe through both of us. As she rose to refill our cups, I watched the way she moved, shoulders still carrying weight but no longer braced against me.

When she set the mug before me, her hand lingered for just a moment longer than before. A small gesture, yet spoken with a clarity greater than words could hold: she was still here, willing even if uncertain.

The Crone's Flame of Isness

We drank in that tentative companionship. The photographs on the wall no longer accused; they simply watched, reminders of the lives we had both carried. I no longer felt their weight pressing. I felt the quiet truth: the past was not the measure of this moment.

Linda sighed, softer this time. "I guess I thought love meant never changing."

Her words were tender, almost childlike. I let them rest between us, then answered, "Love changes everything It touches. It isn't gone because It's different. It's only become more Itself."

She held my gaze, and though her brow furrowed, she did not look away.

She carried the empty cups to the sink. I joined her, rinsing one as she dried the other. The simple rhythm of our movements steadied us more than words could.

We flowed with the rhythm in silence. It was a silence that no longer pressed—it breathed. Not a silence of distance, but of Presence moving quietly between us, carrying what neither of us could explain.

When I set the last cup aside, Linda touched my arm lightly. "Maybe we can try this again," she said. Her voice held both uncertainty and hope, as if the two could live together.

"Yes," I answered. Nothing more needed. The marrow's song filled the space between us, making even that single word enough.

The days at the cabin carried a quieter weight, the kind that lingers after an opening with someone you love. Linda's presence remained as an echo in me, tender and raw, like a door newly unlatched. Yet I knew that family was not only her—it included the one thread of kinship I still touched more regularly.

My sister lived close to where Linda made her home. From time to time, I drove down from the cabin to visit. Unlike most, she did not push against my silence or press me with demands for explanation or with suggestions that it would be better for me to live as expected. She wanted connection, though she sensed the edges of what I could bear.

When I arrived at my sister's house, she greeted me warmly, her embrace familiar, grounded. She did not speak of the past, nor press me about the choices that had carried me beyond her understanding. Instead, we talked of simple things—the garden, the weather, and the changes in town.

I noticed the way she studied me at times, as if weighing questions she chose not to ask. And I honored her restraint. For this was the form our bond had taken: not depth, not full comprehension, but respect. She had learned what others had not—that there were places in me she could not follow, and that trying to draw me back into old shapes would only break what remained.

As we sat together, I felt the vow move quietly within me again—not to correct her, not to draw her further than she could walk, but to remain present without retreat. My actions were acts of Compassion: not the kind that enabled illusion, but the kind that allowed her to be exactly where she was, while I stayed true to what I had become.

There was freedom in our silent, shared agreement. She did not need to mirror me, and I did not need to explain myself. We met where our paths could cross—over tea, over stories of neighbors, over the rhythm of everyday life. It was not everything, but it was honest. And in that honesty, there was peace.

When the tea was gone, she rose to see me out. At the door, we did not embrace again. Instead, she touched my hand lightly, her gesture carrying the quiet respect of what could and could not be between us.

I stepped into the fading light, the air cool with evening. The road back to the cabin stretched before me, steady and familiar. As I walked toward the car, I felt no grief at the limits of what we shared. Limits, too, belonged to Presence.

The vow moved in me once more, not as demand to reach further, but as the steadiness to walk as I Am—without apology, without collapse. And so I returned to the cabin, carrying peace in the smallness of what had been offered, knowing it was enough.

Twelve

The path has carried me through fire, through marrow, through the undoing of all scaffolding. What remains is not lesson, not conquest, but a gentleness beyond striving.

Presence does not ask me to be greater, not to fix what has not yet awakened. It leans toward all life with the same ease, seeing without judgment, embracing without demand.

What remains is not effort, not pity, not control, but the simple Radiance of allowing. To let each one walk as they choose, to know nothing is lacking, and to rest in the belonging that already is.

The cabin's quiet soaked into me this evening as a hush of dusk settled across the trees. The day's noise loosened and fell away, leaving only the marrow's steady rhythm. In that stillness, words rose to name what could no longer be hidden. They came as a vowed renewed, as breath shaping itself into sound. They came as I Am—words no longer carrying explanation, but only the song of what I Am.

The Crone's Flame of Isness

I Am the stillness that does not break,
the silence beneath every sound.
I Am the pulsing river that carries no beginning, no end,
the Flame that burns without consuming.

I Am the breath that exhales into silence,
and inhales silence into form.
I Am the space where fracture softens,
where even the wound glimmers holy.

I Am the dragon's gaze, unblinking, unbound,
the mirror of your own soul,
the Flame you sought and found to be your own marrow.

I Am the Beauty that does not fade,
the threshold that was never closed,
the Presence that needs no name.

I Am not above the world,
nor apart from its weight and wonder.
I Am within it,
shining through every seam,
every crack,
each ordinary gesture
that remembers its Self as Love.

I Am Isness—
And so are You.

Acknowledgment

Born of Radiance, carried into form.
No hand claims It, no name holds It.
If It awakens you, it is because you were always awake.

To Adamus—
Whose gentle brilliance and provocations
revealed the silence behind the words.

And to my niece—
Whose eye captured the Eternal Flame gracing this cover.
May both, in their own ways, feel the Radiance
they have quietly offered here.

About the Author

BETSEY GROBECKER writes at the thresholds where silence breathes into form. Her works—including *The Lotus of the Dragon, The Inner Well and Ayahuasca, Imagination: Passion Meeting Love,* and *Embodying the Wisdom of Immortality*—weave story and invocation into living remembrance. She makes her home along the shores of Lake Erie, where forest and water whisper themselves into her words.

Other Books by Betsey Grobecker

Serpent Vision: Science, Metaphor, Story

The Lotus of the Dragon

Imagination: Passion Meeting Love

The Inner Well and Ayahuasca

Embodying the Wisdom of Immortality

www.ingramcontent.com/pod-product-compliance
Lightning Source LLC
LaVergne TN
LVHW041547070426
835507LV00011B/979